I moved.
I've moved once every two years since I came to Tokyo. My parents and editor think I just like moving, but I don't. I just get tired of things quickly and after two years I feel like going somewhere else.

–Tite Kubo

Bleach is author Tite Kubo's second title. Kubo made his debut with *ZOMBIEPOWDER.*, a four-volume series for *Weekly Shonen Jump*. To date, *Bleach* has been translated into numerous languages and has also inspired an animated TV series that began airing in the U.S. in 2006. Beginning its serialization in 2001, *Bleach* is still a mainstay in the pages of *Weekly Shonen Jump*. In 2005, *Bleach* was awarded the prestigious Shogakukan Manga Award in the *shonen* (boys) category.

D0377927

BLEACH
Vol. 26: The Mascaron Drive
The SHONEN JUMP Manga Edition

This volume contains material that was originally published in SHONEN JUMP #72-74. Artwork in the magazine may have been altered slightly from what is presented in this volume.

STORY AND ART BY
TITE KUBO

English Adaptation/Lance Caselman
Translation/Joe Yamazaki
Touch-Up Art & Lettering/Mark McMurray
Design/Sean Lee
Editor/Pancha Diaz

Editor in Chief, Books/Alvin Lu
Editor in Chief, Magazines/Marc Weidenbaum
VP, Publishing Licensing/Rika Inouye
VP, Sales & Product Marketing/Gonzalo Ferreyra
VP, Creative/Linda Espinosa
Publisher/Hyoe Narita

BLEACH © 2001 by Tite Kubo. All rights reserved. First published in Japan in 2001 by SHUEISHA Inc., Tokyo. English translation rights arranged by SHUEISHA Inc. The stories, characters and incidents mentioned in this publication are entirely fictional.

No portion of this book may be reproduced or transmitted in any form or by any means without written permission from the copyright holders.

The rights of the author(s) of the work(s) in this publication to be so identified have been asserted in accordance with the Copyright, Designs and Patents Act 1988. A CIP catalogue record for this book is available from the British Library.

Printed in the U.S.A.

Published by VIZ Media, LLC
P.O. Box 77010
San Francisco, CA 94107

SHONEN JUMP Manga Edition
10 9 8 7 6 5 4 3 2 1
First printing, March 2009

VIZ media
www.viz.com

RATED T FOR TEEN
PARENTAL ADVISORY
BLEACH is rated T for Teen and is recommended for ages 13 and up. This volume contains fantasy violence.
ratings.viz.com

THE WORLD'S MOST POPULAR MANGA
SHONEN JUMP
www.shonenjump.com

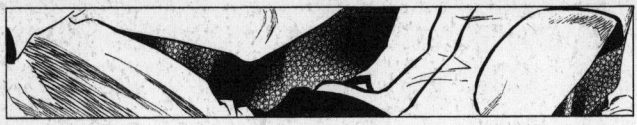

The voice that pierces deep into my chest Is like a never-ending cheer.

BLEACH 26

THE MASCARON DRIVE

Shonen Jump Manga

STARS AND

井上織姫

Orihime Inoue

Rukia Kuchiki

朽木ルキア

Ichigo Kurosaki

黒崎一護

When Ichigo Kurosaki meets Soul Reaper Rukia Kuchiki his life is changed forever, and soon Ichigo becomes a Soul Reaper himself. When Rukia is taken back to the Soul Society for execution, Ichigo saves her and exposes the sinister plot of Sôsuke Aizen in the process. But Aizen escapes to Hueco Mundo, and Ichigo returns to the World of the Living and resumes his work as a Soul Reaper.

Just when Ichigo's life has returned to abnormal, a group of Arrancars–Hollows with the powers of Soul Reapers–makes a foray to his own hometown. The Soul Society, anticipating a large-scale invasion, sends a detachment of Soul Reapers, including Rukia, to the World of the Living. But it soon becomes clear that Aizen's true goal is to create an Ôken, a key that will allow him to assassinate the king of the Soul Society! While Ichigo trains to ready himself for the Arrancars, Orihime races to bring him the news that Karakura is in danger of total destruction!!

BLEACH ALL STORIES

ウルキオラ
Ulquiorra

浦原喜助
Kisuke Urahara

Grimmjow
グリムジョー

BLEACH 26

THE MASCARON DRIVE

Contents

224. Imitated Gaiety 7
225. Slip into My Barrier 27
226. Right of My Heart 45
227. The Swordless Soldier 63
228. Don't Look Back 83
229. The Howling Tempest 103
230. Dead White Invasion 125
231. The Mascaron Drive 145
232. The Mascaron Drive 2 164
233. El Violador 185

224. Imitated Gaiety

TM P
MOMO!

TÔSHIRÔ...
...

...BUT IT MAY HAVE BEEN A BIT TOO SOON.
I'M SORRY.
I GRANTED HER REQUEST TO SPEAK WITH YOU...
SWUMP
THANK YOU.
IT'S ALL RIGHT, SIR.
ZZ T
GOODBYE, SIR.
CAPTAIN HITSUGAYA ...
KRK
KSHHHHHHHHHHH

AIZEN.

224. Imitated Gaiety

CHAK

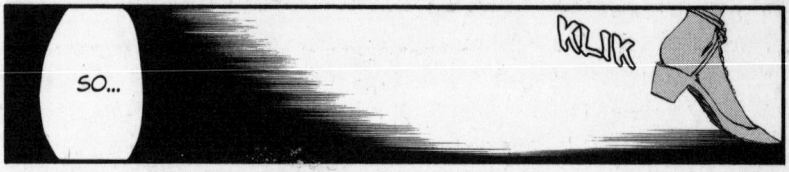
SO...
KLIK

ARE YOU SURE YOU SHOULD BE UP AND AROUND?

YOU'RE AWAKE.
MOMO...

FORGIVE ME.

I'M SORRY I DOUBTED YOU.

I'M SORRY ...
...I DREW MY SWORD AGAINST YOU.
I DON'T KNOW WHAT I WAS THINKING.
I'M SUCH A--
STOP.
I'VE ALREADY FORGOTTEN ABOUT IT.
IT'S BEHIND US.
IT DOESN'T MATTER.
JUST FORGET ABOUT IT. GO BACK TO SLEEP...
...AND GET RID OF THOSE BAGS UNDER YOUR EYES.

...YOU ALREADY LOOK LIKE A KID.
AND CHILDREN NEED TWICE AS MUCH SLEEP AS GROWN-UPS OR THEY STOP GROWING.
THANK YOU, TÔSHIRÔ.
BE-CAUSE YOU KNOW...
ALL RIGHT.

SHUT UP!
RANGIKU'S A FREAK OF NATURE!
YOU NEED AT LEAST 10 YEARS OF SLEEP TO CATCH UP WITH HER.
LOOK AT MATSU-MOTO.

DON'T MAKE ME REPEAT MYSELF.
MOMO!
WHO ARE YOU TO GIVE SOMEBODY ELSE ADVICE ABOUT GROWING ANYWAY?!

I'M CAPTAIN HITSUGAYA.
I'M NOT TÔSHIRÔ NOW...

YES.
OF COURSE.

...

CAP-TAIN ...
CAN I ASK YOU SOME-THING?
WHAT?
46

...CAPTAIN AIZEN?
ARE YOU GOING TO FIGHT...

ARE YOU GOING TO...
...KILL HIM?

...
YES.
46

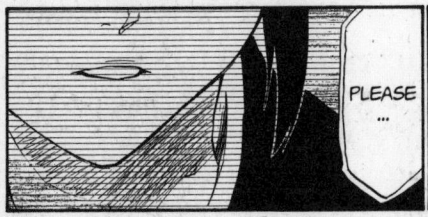
PLEASE ...

...CAPTAIN AIZEN!
DON'T KILL...

THAT'S IT!
MAYBE CAPTAIN ICHIMARU OR SOMEONE FORCED HIM TO--

MOMO!

I KNOW HE DID SOME TERRIBLE THINGS...
BUT HE MUST'VE HAD A REASON!
WHUP

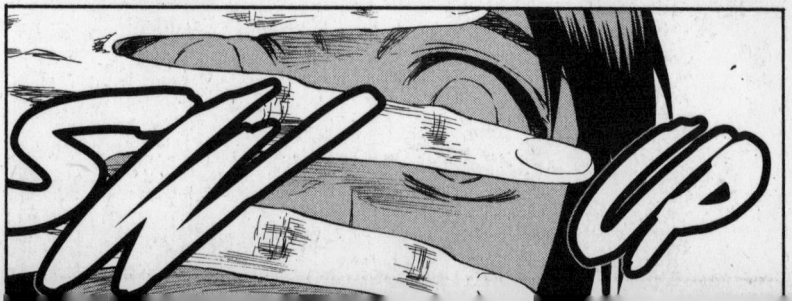
SWIP

WHAT'S WRONG ?!
YOU'RE GETTING WEAK!!
NO...
I'M NOT!

HELP HIM TRAIN?!

*BREAKDOWN SPHERE. ALLOWS ARRANCARS TO BE INSTANTANEOUSLY CREATED FROM HOLLOWS.

OH, YES. I FORGOT. ♪
LET ME GO!!
I'VE NEVER MET ANYONE SO FRUSTRATING BEFORE IN MY LIFE!!
I'LL MANGLE HIM!!
IT HAS TO BE YOU.
MY BANKAI ISN'T SUITED...
...FOR TRAINING OR GIVING PEOPLE STRENGTH.
...
AHA!
I'VE GOT IT!
HOW ABOUT THIS?
THERE'S SOMETHING YOU WANT TO ASK ME, RIGHT?
UP TO NOW I'VE MANAGED TO WORM MY WAY OUT OF IT, BUT...
GEEZ, YOU'RE LAZY.
LET'S MAKE A DEAL!
IF YOU AGREE TO DO ODD JOBS FOR ME FOR THE NEXT THREE MONTHS...
...I'LL ANSWER ANY QUESTIONS YOU ASK!

...GIVE UP ON THAT THING YOU WANT TO ASK ME?
OR WOULD YOU RATHER...
IT'S A NUISANCE AND ONE COULD GET KILLED DOING IT.
SURE IT IS!
TRAINING SOMEONE IN BANKAI ISN'T AN ODD JOB!
TR-

YEAH.
HE TRICKED HIM INTO DOING ODD JOBS ON TOP OF THE TRAINING?
STUPID PINE-APPLE HEAD.
FINE.
I'LL DO IT!

WOOOOOOOO
...HE CERTAINLY IS THROWING HIMSELF INTO IT.
SWASH
CONSIDERING HOW RESISTANT HE WAS...
WHAM

MR. SADO...
YOUR POWERS CLEARLY HAVE THE POTENTIAL TO INCREASE.

REPEATED BATTLES AGAINST BANKAI WILL RAISE THEM TO NEW HEIGHTS.
BUT ONE THING TROUBLES ME...

YOUR POWERS AREN'T LIKE THOSE OF SOUL REAPERS OR QUINCIES...
YES. IT'S AS IF YOUR POWERS ARE...

AAAA AAH!!
KR AK
OOF!!
CHK AK
I TOLD YOU TO STAY HOLLOWFIED, BALDY!!

THEY'RE GETTING ALONG SWIM-MINGLY.
YEAH.
WHAT ?!
IDIOT!! THAT'S THE WHOLE POINT OF THIS TRAINING! IF YOU'RE NOT GONNA DO IT RIGHT, THEN DON'T DO IT AT ALL!!
ARE YOU STUPID OR SOME-THING?! I'D BE IN BIG TROUBLE IF I'D STAYED HOLLOW-FIED!!

WOOOOOOOOO
TMP

THAT HAS TO BE IT.
...

...LET'S TAKE A TRIP TO THE WORLD OF THE LIVING AND GO TO THE BEACH!
YEAH.
WE COULD ALL USE A LITTLE BREAK, SO...
A TRIP ?!
SOCIETY OF FEMALE SOUL REAPERS CHAIRWOMAN: RETSU UNOHANA

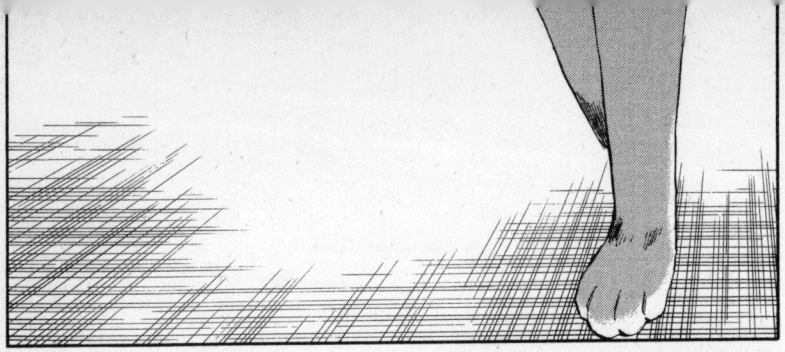

225. Slip into My Barrier

...BECAUSE THERE'S A FORCE FIELD THERE.
THEY CAN'T GO NEAR IT...
AMAZING.
THEY CAN'T EVEN THINK OF APPROACHING IT.
IT'S BLOCKING THIS BUILDING OUT OF PEOPLE'S MINDS. THEY DON'T EVEN KNOW IT'S HERE.

TIN
G

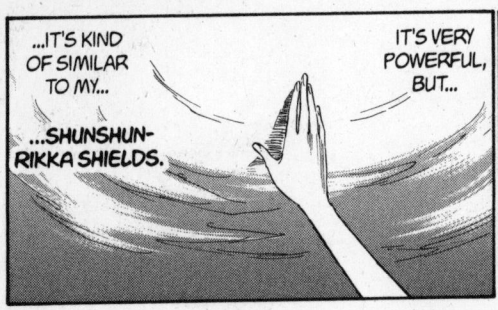
...IT'S KIND OF SIMILAR TO MY...
...SHUNSHUN-RIKKA SHIELDS.
IT'S VERY POWERFUL, BUT...

BUT...
IT'S STRANGE.

VWM

I CAN PUT MY HAND THROUGH IT.
...

BLEACH 225. Slip into My Barrier

SHUT UP! I KNOW !!
ONE MORE TIME!!
COME ON, ICHIGO!
TM
P
F
UP
WM
M

WHAK
OW!!
HOW MANY TIMES DO I HAVE TO TELL YOU--YOU'RE SLOWER IMMEDIATELY AFTER YOU HOLLOWFY !!
IF THAT FIRST BLOW OF MINE HAD LANDED, YOU'D BE DEAD!!
TOMP TOMP TOMP TOMP TOMP

KROOM KROOM

KRAS H

THWAK

KRE ES

WELL, IT'S NOT EASY.
HIS RETENTION TIME ISN'T INCREASING VERY QUICKLY.

SO, HEY...
...DOING THIS ANY-WAY?
WHY'S BERRY BOY...
WHOA, THAT'S SHORT!
FOUR SECONDS.

IT'S TRUE.
WHAT? LIAR.
NO, I DIDN'T.
HE'S TRAINING TO INCREASE THE LENGTH OF TIME THAT HE CAN REMAIN HOLLOW-FIED.
YOU DID IT TOO.

SHE'S THE ONLY ONE WHO HASN'T DONE THIS PART OF THE TRAINING.
MASHIRO WAS ABLE TO HOLLOWFY FOR OVER 15 HOURS FROM THE VERY START.

KRAK
NOW, NOW...
WHY, YOU!!
KENSEI, YOU GROUCH!
YOU'RE A JERK!
SEE?!
BLEH
HMPH
REALLY?
GUESS I FORGOT.

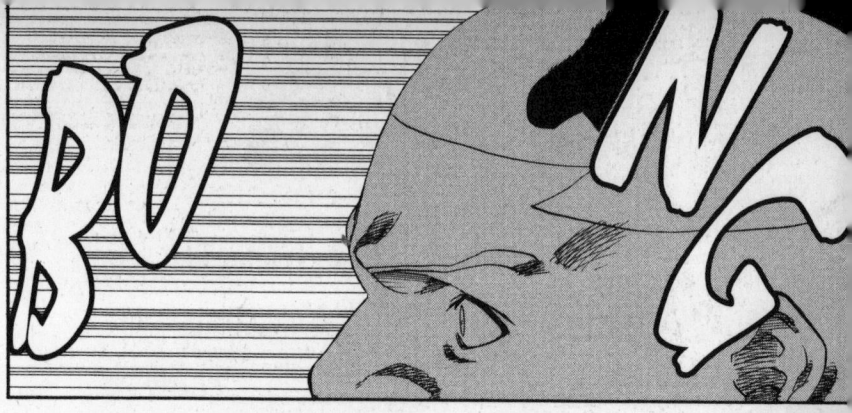
BO
NG

WHAT'S UP, HACHI?
WH
UP

SOME-ONE...
...JUST SLIPPED THROUGH MY FORCE FIELD.

!!!!

THE HACHIGYÔ SÔGAI (TWIN CLIFFS) I SET IS AN ORIGINAL TECHNIQUE I DEVELOPED AFTER I BECAME A VISORED.
IT CAN'T BE BROKEN BY A SOUL REAPER'S KIDÔ.

A SOUL REAPER?
NO.

THEN...
...WHO OR **WHAT** IS IT?

THEN WHO IS IT?! ANOTHER VISORED?!
I DON'T KNOW.
NOT EVEN A VISORED SHOULD BE ABLE TO DO THAT.
THE STRANGE THING IS THAT THEY DIDN'T BREAK THROUGH THE FORCE FIELD. THEY **SLIPPED** THROUGH.

TM
P

IT'S COM-ING.

...

SHWO

STARE

IT'S A...
...HUMAN ?!

UH...
UM...

GRR
HUH?!
IF IT WERE ME, I WOULDN'T BE JOKING AROUND IN A SITUATION LIKE THIS.
SHE SAID SHE WAS KIDDING.
WHAT DO YOU THINK, KENSEI?
THAT WAS A JOKE.
E-EXCUSE ME...
WHERE'S THE BATHROOM?
JUST KIDDING.

THUD
!

KRUNCH
UGH!
CRAP ...
WHAT ARE YOU DOING, ICHIGO?!

ORIHIME ?!

ICHIGO !!

...
I SEE.

?
WHAT?

...

OH...
I MEAN...
YOU DON'T SEEM VERY SURPRISED BY WHAT I TOLD YOU.

TMP
BUT IT'S OKAY.

...I JUST FOUND OUT THAT KARAKURA'S GOING TO BE WIPED OUT BECAUSE OF THIS ÔKEN THING, AND... I'M JUST HAVING A HARD TIME WRAPPING MY HEAD AROUND IT.
IT'S JUST THAT...
SURE I AM.

DON'T WORRY.
I'M GONNA STOP AIZEN.

I'M GETTING STRONGER.
I CAN...
...FEEL IT.

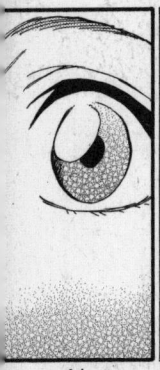

THANKS FOR THE HEADS-UP...
...ORI-HIME.

...BECAUSE HE'S SO BUSY TRAINING AND GETTING STRONGER.
HE CAN'T REALLY PROCESS WHAT I TOLD HIM...
THAT'S MS. HIYORI, BALDY!!
ALL RIGHT!
LET'S GET BACK TO TRAINING, HIYORI!
I SEE.

HE'S NOT AFRAID.
ICHIGO KNOWS EXACTLY WHAT HE HAS TO DO.
IT DOESN'T MATTER WHAT AIZEN IS PLANNING.

...AND NOT IN A SCARY WAY LIKE BEFORE...
...GETTING REALLY STRONG...
ICHIGO'S...

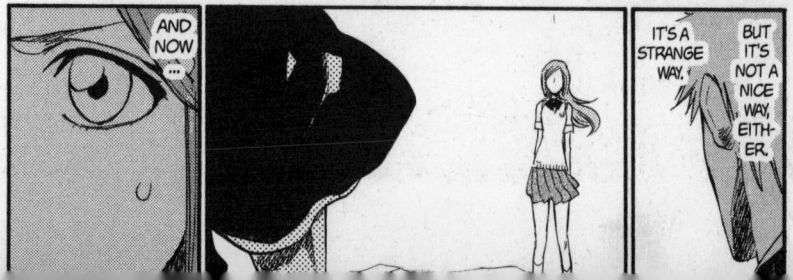
AND NOW ...
IT'S A STRANGE WAY.
BUT IT'S NOT A NICE WAY, EITHER.

...GET STRONGER TOO!
I HAVE TO...
TMP

CALL ME CHAIR-WOMAN HERE.
HERE?! WE'RE IN THE BAR-RACKS!
WA...
WAIT, CAPTAIN UNO-HANA!
...IN THE WORLD OF THE LIVING!
WHAT?
THEN LET'S GO BUY YOU ONE RIGHT NOW...
OH, NO!
IT'S A SIZE ISSUE.
I DON'T HAVE A BATHING SUIT.
WHY NOT?
UM...
THAT SOUNDS LIKE FUN, BUT I CAN'T GO.

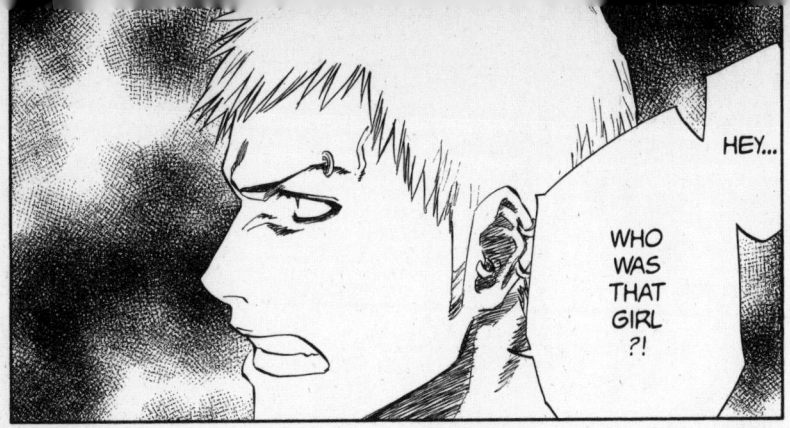

226: Right of My Heart

WHOA!!
DON'T TAKE YOUR EYES OFF ME!!
THAT'S BECAUSE I DIDN'T, DIPSTICK.
HE SAYS THAT ABOUT EVERY PRETTY GIRL?!
I DON'T REMEMBER HIM SAYING THAT ABOUT ME!!

YES?
HACHI...

OF COURSE.

YOUR FORCE FIELDS ARE FLAW-LESS.
THERE'S NO DOUBT ABOUT THAT.

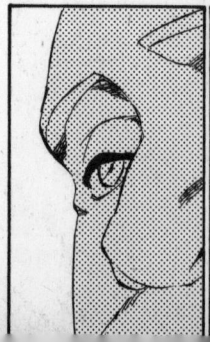

...AND GET INSIDE?
THEN HOW DID ORIHIME DETECT THIS PLACE...

...I BELIEVE SHE POSSESSES THE SAME TYPE OF FORCE FIELD ABILITY THAT I DO.
I COULD FEEL IT.
BOOM
KRASH
HAVING EXAMINED HER SPIRITUAL PRESSURE AT CLOSE RANGE...
KRASH
I'M NOT SURE.
HOW-EVER ...

...AND SLIP THROUGH MY FORCE FIELD.
THAT ABILITY ALLOWED HER TO DETECT THIS PLACE...

...THAT A HUMAN COULD HAVE SUCH POWERS.
THOUGH IT SEEMS INCREDIBLE...

WOO
THERE YOU ARE...
...ORI-HIME.

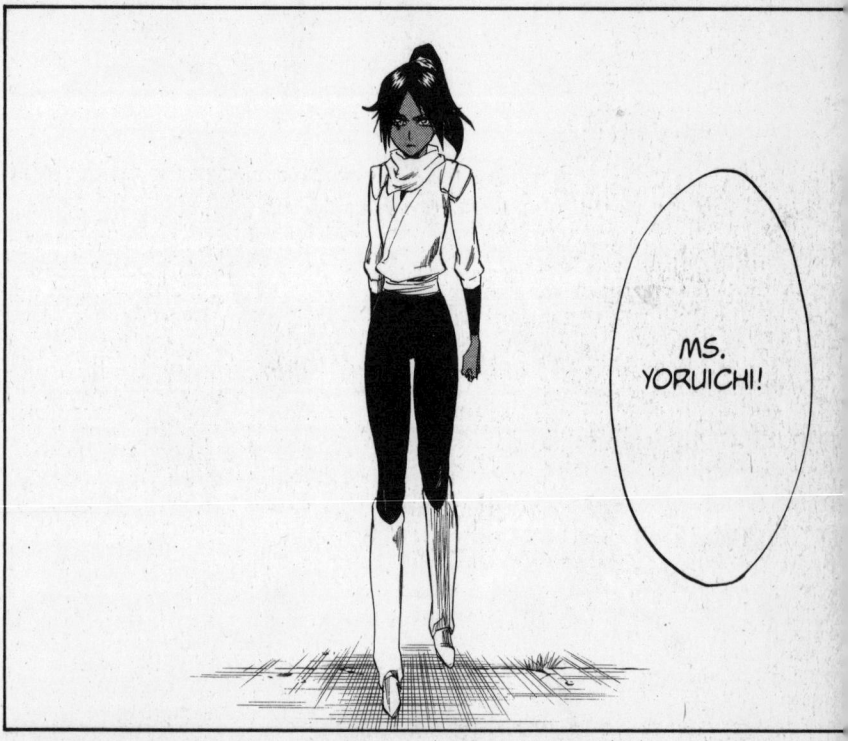
MS. YORUICHI!

KISUKE SENT ME...
...TO FIND YOU.

BLEACH

226. Right of My Heart

HUFF
HUFF
HUFF
HUFF

DA-DA-DA-DA-DA-DOON
KEEEN
HUFF

!
SWIP
WHUP
SH...
SHOOT!
THOOM
TILT THE GOBLET TO THE WEST!
WOLKE!! (EMERALD CHALICE)
WOOSH

KKMMMMMMMMMMMM
SO YOU HAD SOME GINTŌ STASHED AWAY.
KLAK
RRMMMM
WOOOO
HUFF
HUFF
ARE YOU CALLING ME...
...A COWARD?
HUFF
WOOOO
HOW VERY CAUTIOUS OF YOU.
MM
EXACTLY.

RRMMMMMMMM
TMP
WHAT'S THE MATTER?
YOU CALL THAT DODGING?!
YOU'RE SLOWING DOWN!
HAVE YOU REACHED YOUR LIMIT?!

FOOM FOOM FOOM FOOM
MY LIMIT?
I CAN BARELY MOVE MY ARMS AND LEGS.
RRMMMM
TMP
TMP
BUT HIS SPIRITUAL PRESSURE IS WEAKENING TOO.
HE TOLD ME THAT IF I KEPT DODGING HIS ARROWS I'D REGAIN MY POWERS, BUT THERE'S NO SIGN THAT IT'S WORKING.
WAS HE LYING TO ME?
BUT IF WE KEEP GOING LIKE THIS, HE'LL KILL ME.

...MY CHANCE!
AND NOW'S ...
I HAVE TO IMMOBILIZE HIM AND END THIS EXERCISE!
I'VE REACHED MY LIMIT.
MY LAST GINTÔ!
TU
!
MP
THE SILVER WHIP STRIKES THE FIVE-FINGERED STONE BED!
TUNK
GRITZ!
(FIVE-PRONGED RESTRAINT)

YES !!
FOOSH
SRIK

WHAT ?!
DO
OM
I'M SORRY.
IT'S OVER.

DO
OM
HE GOT ME.
UGH...

THUD
YOU HAVE TO PUSH YOUR MIND AND BODY TO THEIR LIMITS...
KLAK
KLAK
KLINK
...BE STRUCK BY A SPIRIT ARROW 19 MM TO THE RIGHT OF THE HEART'S SINOATRIAL NODE.
KLAK
...AND WHILE IN THAT CONDITION ...

THAT...
...IS THE ONLY WAY TO REGAIN THE SPIRITUAL POWERS LOST WHILE IN...
...QUINCY LETZ STILE. (FINAL FORM)

...YOU MAY NOT HAVE DEFEATED ME, BUT YOU MIGHT'VE AT LEAST INFLICTED A WOUND.
IF YOU'D USED HAIZEN INSTEAD OF GRITZ...
TMP
WHY DIDN'T YOU USE HAIZEN?
WHY?

YOU MAKE ME SICK.
YOU MADE A STUPID CHOICE.

BUT...
I'LL LET YOU LIVE THIS TIME.

I'D BETTER GO BUY A NEW SWIM-SUIT.
SERIOUSLY ?!
YAY!! WATERMELON!!
THE BEACH ?!

227. The Swordless Soldier

HA HA HA HA HA HA HA!!
ZA NG

I GOT THIS FROM THE LANDLADY!
BUT MORE IMPORTANTLY...
...WHAT HAS THIS WORLD DONE TO YOUR FASHION SENSE?

M-M-MATSUMOTO?! HOW'D YOU GET IN HERE?!
THE FRONT DOOR.
IT WAS OPEN.
DON'T YOU HAVE ANY SECURITY IN THIS PLACE?

YOU JUST WEAR WHATEVER THE LANDLADY GIVES YOU?!
OF COURSE!!
WE'VE GOT FREE ROOM AND BOARD HERE! YOU THINK I'M GONNA COMPLAIN ABOUT THE CLOTHES SHE GIVES ME?!

READ THIS WAY
YOU KNOW. THAT GIRL.
ORIHIME.
SHE MAY BE A MORTAL, BUT EVEN I'M STARTING TO FEEL SORRY FOR HER.
WHO'S THE POOR SUCKER SHE'S STAYING WITH?
REALLY ?
I COMPLAIN LIKE CRAZY. ABOUT THE FOOD, THE CLOTHES...
MR. IKKAKU, MR. YUMI-CHIKA...
HOW IS EVERY-
-THING?
KREEK
HELLO...
I'M HOME!
CHAK
I MUST BE DREAMING! IT'S THE SECOND COMING OF THE GODDESS OF BREASTS!!
EVEN CLOTHES CAN'T HIDE THEM! OH, THE NAUGHTI-NESS!!
YAHOO!!
DOOM

WHAM
SHRSHHH
!
HEH HEH... I'VE BEEN UNDER-ESTIMATED.
I, KEIGO ASANO...
...WILL NEVER FALL FOR THE SAME TECHNI--
GACK!!

SLAM
HONEY, I'M HOME!
HAVE YOU BEEN A GOOD BOY?!
KLUNK
HEY...
TAKE IT EASY ON THE BOY. HE ONLY WANTED TO JUMP YOU.
OH...
SORRY. REFLEX.
SORRY.
WRONG DOOR.
HEY, WAIT A MINUTE!!
I COULDN'T MISTAKE MY OWN HOUSE! WHO THE HECK ARE YOU PEOPLE?!
IS EVERYONE AROUND HERE LIKE THEM?
LOOK, IT'S GOING TO GET MESSY, SO DO WHAT YOU CAME HERE TO DO AND GO.
WHAT DO YOU WANT?
SHIN
UP

BLEACH 227. The Swordless Soldier

HARA SHÔTEN
WELL...
HELLO THERE, MS. INOUE!
IT'S BEEN A LONG TIME. ♪
UH-HUH...

WHAM
KRASH
PLEASE, PLEASE!
HAVE A SEAT!
OOF
WELL, I'VE BEEN WATCHING TWO SWEATY GUYS WAIL ON EACH OTHER FOR DAYS NOW...
...SO IT'S NICE HAVING A YOUNG WOMAN STOP BY THE OFFICE.

WHAM
AGH!!
UM...
MR. URA-HARA...

RENJI?
CHAD?

KLAK
KLAK
KLAK

TUMP

TESSAI! URURU!
CHAD!
WHUP

URA-HARA !!
HE'S EXHAUST-ED!
I'M CALLING IT A DAY!

WA...
WAIT.
KLAK

PLEASE REVIVE CHAD.
!

YOU'RE PUSHING YOUR-SELF TOO HARD, TOUGH GUY.
KLAK
I CAN ...
...KEEP GOING.

MR. URA-HARA ...

RAN-GIKU...
...OF TENTH COMPANY STOPPED BY EARLIER.
WHAT IS IT ...
...YOU WANTED TO TALK TO ME ABOUT?

IT CAUGHT US ALL BY SURPRISE, I'M AFRAID.
WE AND THE SOUL SOCIETY HAVE TO PREPARE TO FIGHT A BATTLE THIS WINTER...
IN ANY CASE...
!
YOU'VE HEARD, HAVEN'T YOU? ABOUT THE ÔKEN?
I'M SURE THE STORY'S REACHED IKKAKU BY NOW AS WELL.

AN ALL-OUT WAR.
A GREAT DEAL OF BLOOD WILL BE SHED, MORE THAN EVER BEFORE.
AND...
...WE'LL ALL NEED TO BE STRONGER THAN EVER BEFORE.

RIGHT.
I...
...WANT TO GET STRONGER TOO!

OF COURSE YOU DO.
BUT THERE'S SOMETHING I HAVE TO TELL YOU.
ORI-HIME ...

YOU WON'T BE...
...FIGHTING WITH US THIS TIME.

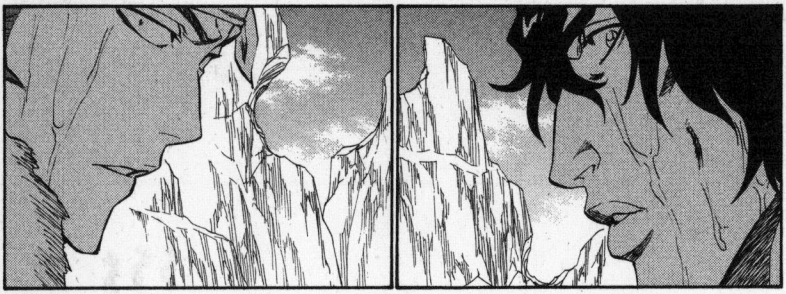

...
WHAT?

TSU-BAKI...
...WAS DESTROYED IN THE BATTLE WITH THE ARRANCARS THE OTHER DAY.
HAS HE BEEN REPAIRED?

...
NO.
HE WAS BROKEN SO BADLY I COULDN'T FIX HIM.
I DON'T EVEN KNOW HOW TO FIX HIM.
TSUBAKI IS YOUR ONLY OFFEN-SIVE WEAPON.
I CAN'T ALLOW YOU TO PARTICIPATE IN THE BATTLE WITHOUT HIM.
IT'S OUT OF THE QUESTION.

SHE'S A FRIEND OF OURS.
SHE FOUGHT HARD IN THE SOUL SOCIETY.

TMP
WHOA...
HOLD ON, MR. URAHARA!

NO!
THAT'S AN EMOTIONAL ARGUMENT.
DO YOU WANT HER TO GET KILLED?

CHAD...
WE CAN'T JUST LEAVE HER BEHIND!
NOW SHE WANTS TO GET STRONGER.

FOURTH COMPANY CAN TAKE CARE OF OUR CASUALTIES.
AND WE'LL HAVE PEOPLE LIKE CAPTAIN UNOHANA AND ASSISTANT CAPTAIN KOTETSU WITH US ON THE FRONT LINES THIS TIME.
THE SANTEN-KESSHUN'S DEFENSIVE CAPABILITIES ARE LIMITED.
IT WON'T BE USEFUL IN THIS UPCOMING BATTLE.

BUT SHE'S GOT AN ABILITY MORE VALUABLE THAN FIGHTING...
SHE CAN PROTECT AND HEAL PEOPLE!

DON'T PESTER ME.
BUT...
...WON'T BE NEEDED.
MS. INOUE'S POWERS...

...WILL ONLY HOLD US BACK.
A WARRIOR THAT CAN'T FIGHT...

THANK YOU, CHAD.
IT'S OKAY, BUT...
?
ORI-HIME ...

IT'S OKAY.
MR. URA-HARA !!

...TOLD ME.
I'M GLAD YOU...
THANK YOU, MR. URAHARA.

GOOD-BYE!

DON'T.
URAHARA'S RIGHT.
RENJI?
WHAP
ORI-HIME!!
DASH

SHE JUST WASN'T MEANT TO BE A WARRIOR.
AND TAKING INTO ACCOUNT HER PERSON-ALITY...
ORIHIME MAY HAVE SOME ABILITIES, BUT SHE'S STILL JUST A HUMAN.
FOURTH COMPANY MAY SPECIALIZE IN HEALING, BUT THEY'VE ALSO HAD COMBAT TRAINING.

ORI-HIME ...
...TO CALL IT QUITS.
MAYBE THIS IS A GOOD TIME FOR HER...

BZZZAK
ZAK

THAT'S AN INTERESTING ABILITY YOU HAVE...

...GIRL.

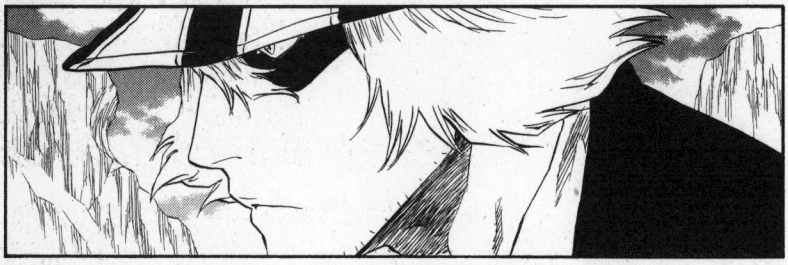

GEEZ... IF YOU'D TOLD ME EARLIER I WOULD'VE PUT SOMETHING LIKE "FAT SOW" ON IT!
I'M BUSY! I DON'T HAVE TIME TO SEW ONE ON FOR YOU!
A NAME-TAG?!
BUT THEN THIS IS A SPECIAL TRIP.
BUT MY BELLY-BUTTON WILL SHOW. HOW EMBAR-RASSING.
HMM... ISN'T IT KIND OF FLASHY?

228. Don't Look Back

ORIHIME?

YOU LOOK SO...
WHAT'S WRONG?

H-HEY! WHAT IS IT, ORIHIME ?!
HUH ?!

RU...
RUKIA...

ORIHIME!!

228. Don't Look Back

WHAT?!

IT'S OKAY.
I FEEL BETTER AFTER TALKING WITH YOU.

URAHARA SAID THAT?! THAT JERK!
YOU POOR THING...
NO.

IT'S NOT OKAY!!

IT'S FOR THE BEST.
HE'S RIGHT. I'M NOT STRONG ENOUGH.

...TO BE DISMISSED LIKE THAT ?!
DOESN'T IT MAKE YOU MAD...
YOU'VE DONE YOUR SHARE OF FIGHTING UP TO NOW!!
YOU EVEN WENT TO THE SOUL SOCIETY AND FOUGHT !!
STOP LYING!!
I...
I'M NOT...
I'M JUST SAD.
I WANT TO FIGHT WITH THE REST OF YOU!
I'M JUST...
AND I'M NOT MAD!
I...
I'M NOT LYING!
IF I'M GOING TO...
...HINDER ICHIGO OR ANYONE ELSE...
...I DON'T WANT TO BE A BURDEN TO ANYONE.
BUT...
...MORE IMPORTANT-LY...

...I'D RATHER BE SAD.

IT'S NOT THE WEAK OF BODY...
...THAT CAUSE PROBLEMS ON THE BATTLE-FIELD.
TMP
LISTEN ...
...ORI-HIME.

IT'S THE WEAK OF SPIRIT.

NOT ONE OF YOU...
...WAS A HINDRANCE IN THE BATTLE AT THE SOUL SOCIETY.
NOT ICHIGO ...
OR CHAD...
OR URYÛ...
AND, ORIHIME...
...NEITHER WERE YOU.
IF ANY ONE OF YOU HADN'T BEEN THERE...
...I'D BE DEAD NOW.
THERE HAS TO BE SOME-THING YOU CAN DO...
...TO MAKE YOURSELF FIT FOR THIS BATTLE.
LET'S FIND IT TOGETHER.
OKAY?
RUKIA...

THUD

HIYORI?!
HI-
WHAT ?!

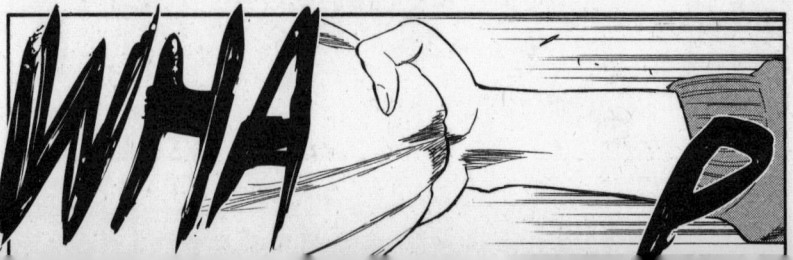
WHAP

READ THIS WAY
YOU'RE COMING WITH ME!
HACHI SAYS HE NEEDS YOU!
WHAT?
WHO'S HACHI?

WA...
WAH!
WA...
SHOOM
WOOOOO
...
WHO...
WHO WAS THAT ?!

THWUMP
OUCH!!

I'M HACHIGEN ISHÔDA...
CALL ME HACHI.
IT'S NICE TO MEET YOU.
STARE
SWAY
HMM...
HMM...
HMM...
...
...NICE TO MEET YOU TOO.
IT'S...
TUMP
UM...
WHAT WAS IT YOU WANTED TO...
OWWWWW!!
MY HEAD! MY HEAD!! YOU'RE GONNA TWIST IT OFF!!

HMM...
AS I SUSPECTED...
THESE HAIR CLIPS ARE THE SOURCE OF YOUR POWER.
THEY'RE ALMOST LIKE ZANPAKUTÔ.
HOW INTERESTING!

!
BUT THIS ONE'S DAMAGED.
IT'S BEEN BOTHERING ME EVER SINCE YOU SHOWED UP HERE.
YES.
I CAN'T FIX IT.
IT GOT BROKEN AND--
WOULD YOU LIKE ME TO FIX IT FOR YOU?

R...
REALLY?!
OF COURSE!

YAY!
THANK YOU!!
YOU'RE WELCOME.
HO HO HO HO HO HO...
THAT'S ENOUGH, HACHI.

I DON'T GET IT!

I THINK HE'S HAPPY.

WHY'S HACHI FIXING HER WEAPON ?!
WHO IS THAT GIRL ANYWAY?! I DON'T LIKE HER!!
STOP WHINING !!
MAKE HER GO AWAY !!

IT PROBABLY ...

WE...
...RARELY MEET ANYONE WITH OUR SAME ABILITIES.

...FEELS LIKE FINDING A LONG-LOST RELATIVE.

...AND PROBABLY OTHERS, AS WELL.

FOR HACHI...

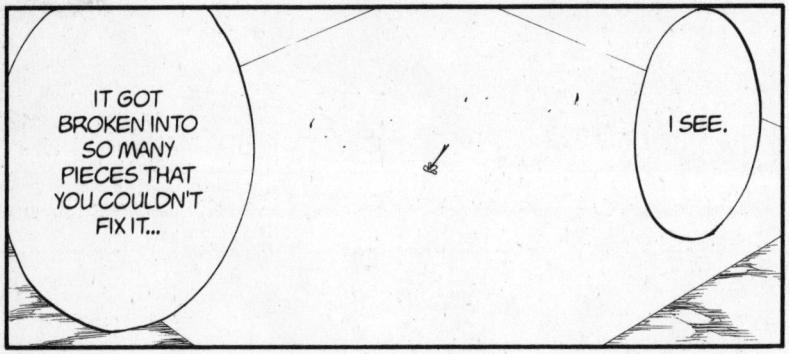
IT GOT BROKEN INTO SO MANY PIECES THAT YOU COULDN'T FIX IT...
I SEE.

AS FAR AS I CAN TELL, YOU POSSESS AN ABILITY VERY MUCH LIKE MY OWN.
BUT IT'S STRANGE.

UM...
NOT EXACTLY, BUT I'VE EXPLAINED IT FIVE TIMES ALREADY SO THAT'S CLOSE ENOUGH.
SO THEY SAID YOU COULDN'T FIGHT.
IS THAT RIGHT?

KEEEEEEEEEE

...RESTORE THESE BROKEN PIECES WITH EASE.
IF SO, YOU SHOULD BE ABLE TO...

POP
TSUBAKI, YOU'RE BACK!!
YAY!!
WHOA!!
WHAT THE?! HEY! LET GO!!
THANK YOU, MR. HACHI!!
SHUKASHUKASHUKA
HUH?
WHAT, WOMAN?
YOU SHOULD SEE YOUR-SELF RIGHT NOW!

ORI-HIME...

NOW THAT TSUBAKI'S FIXED...
...YOU SHOULD BE ABLE TO JOIN THE BATTLE LINE.

BUT I...
...WOULD ADVISE YOU NOT TO.

DO YOU STILL...
...WANT TO FIGHT?

IF YOUR ABILITY IS LIKE MINE...
...YOU'RE NOT SUITED FOR COMBAT ...
...ESPECIALLY AGAINST THE ARRANCARS.

YES.
I WANT TO FIGHT!

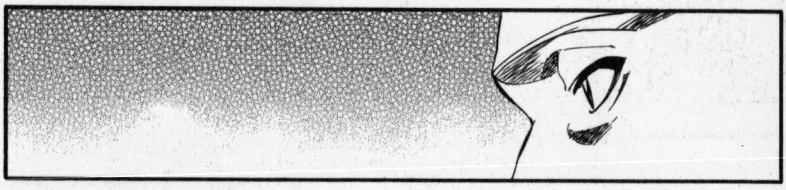

THEN YOU SHALL.
BUT YOU DON'T FULLY UNDER-STAND YOUR ABILITIES YET.
THERE IS A WAY FOR YOU TO FIGHT, BUT YOU MUST FIND IT.
PLEASE REMEMBER THIS...

...THE IMPORTANT THING ISN'T HOW YOU SHOULD BE...
...BUT HOW YOU WANT TO BE.

THANK YOU!

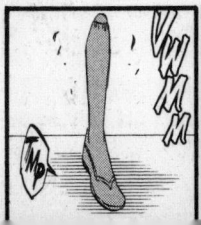
MMM
TMP

RUKIA!

I CAME HERE BECAUSE I SENSED A TRACE OF ICHIGO'S SPIRITUAL PRESSURE.
IF HE HASN'T TOLD ME ABOUT THIS, I'M SURE THERE'S A GOOD REASON.
AS LONG AS HE'S SAFE...
...THAT'S ENOUGH FOR ME.

UM...
YOU SEE, RUKIA ?!
DON'T TELL ME.
I DON'T WANT TO KNOW.
INSIDE THERE'S A-

LET'S GO...
...ORI-HIME.

BUT I WON'T TURN TO YOU THIS TIME.

I'M WEAK, SO I ALWAYS TURN TO YOU.
ICHIGO...

...I'LL BE ABLE TO FIGHT WITHOUT LOOKING AT YOUR BACK.
THE NEXT TIME WE SEE EACH OTHER...

YEAH.
LET'S GO, RUKIA.

SOI FON!
I FOUND ONE FOR YOU TOO!
GASP!
WHAT AM I DOING?! I NEED TO GET ONE FOR ME!
OH! EXCELLENT CHOICE!
YOU LOOK SO ELEGANT PICKING OUT A SWIM-SUIT!!
HMM... I'M GOING WITH THIS ONE!

229. The Howling Tempest

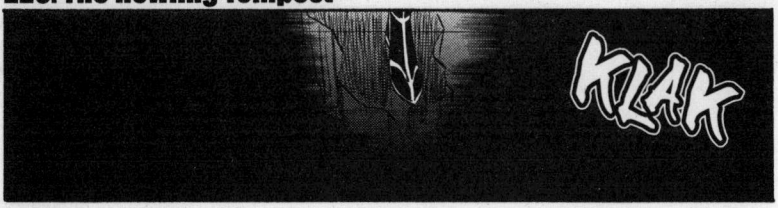

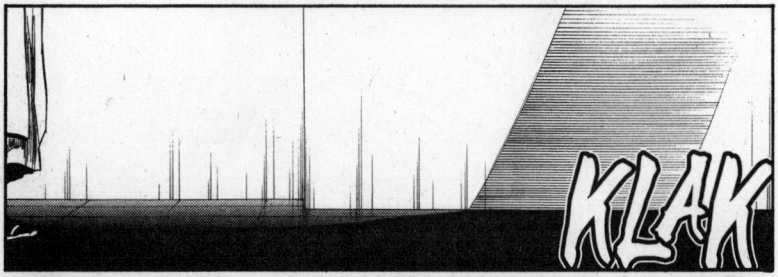

GREEEK

...
IS THAT YOU, ULQUI-ORRA?
WHAT DO YOU WANT?

YOU'VE HEALED.
GOOD THING WE BROUGHT BACK YOUR SEVERED ARM.

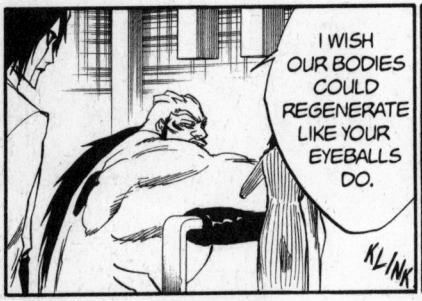
I WISH OUR BODIES COULD REGENERATE LIKE YOUR EYEBALLS DO.
KLINK

WHAT TOOK SO LONG?
SNIK
KLINK...
SNIK
I THOUGHT MY ARM WAS GONNA ROT.

STOP COMPLAINING.
AT LEAST IT'S BACK ON.
IF YOUR ARM HAD BEEN COMPLETELY DESTROYED, LIKE GRIMMJOW'S WAS...
...YOU WOULD'VE BEEN DROPPED FROM THE ESPADAS TOO.

HMPH...

MAYBE.

THE TREAT-MENT ...
...IS COM-PLETE.
GOOD.
WHUP
WHUP
HOW IS IT, SIR?
IS THERE ANY LOSS OF MOBILITY OR SENSITIVITY COMPARED TO BEFORE THE DISMEMBER-MENT?
HUH?

READ THIS WAY
FWSHHH
FWUP
SPLAK
TMP
WHERE ARE WE GOING ?
STUPID.
LET'S GO.
SP
LAT
IT'S NO GOOD.
THAT WOULD'VE SPLIT HER IN TWO IF I WAS AT MY BEST.

MASTER AIZEN WANTS TO SEE US.
BLEACH
229. The Howling Tempest
BOOM
October 29, Karakura: Underground Headquarters of the Vizards

FWUMP
HE'S TELLING THESE GUYS THEY'RE DEAD...
...BUT THEY JUST DON'T REALIZE IT YET.
THAT'S SUCH A DEEP LINE, HUH?
"YOU'RE ALREADY DEAD."
KR EESH
AND WILL YOU STOP READING MY COMICS BEFORE I DO? YOU SPOIL EVERY-THING?
IS THAT SUPPOSED TO SOUND LIKE WHAT SCHIELE* SAID OR SOME-THING?
THWAM
THWAM
JUST LIKE THAT.
DON'T YOU SEE?
YOU'RE ALIVE AND THEY'RE DEAD...
*Egon Schiele. A German Expressionist painter who said: "Everything is dead while it lives."
KLAK
YOU THOUGHT SOUL REAPERS WERE SUPPOSED TO GET KILLED A LOT, RIGHT?!
OH, I GET IT!
WELL YOU'RE WRONG, BALDY!!
SHUT...
...UP!
DO YOU KNOW HOW MANY TIMES I COULD'VE KILLED YOU?!
GET UP, FOOL!!
KLA NK

LAST ONE IN LINE HAS TO DO THE DISHES!!
CHOW TIME!!
GET YOUR BUTTS OVER HERE!!
OOH!

YOU LITTLE ...
SKRUSH
SKRUSH
SKRUSH
BALDY'S A JOKE.
HE'S ONLY UP TO A LITTLE OVER TEN SECONDS.
WEREN'T YOU WATCHING?
HE'S DOG MEAT.
IT'S NOT GOING ANY-WHERE.

SO?
HOW'S ICHIGO'S TRAINING GOING, HIYORI?
SKRUSH
SKRUSH SKRUSH

I LENT YOU THAT GIRLIE MAGAZINE THE OTHER DAY, REMEMBER?!
YES I AM, MORON !!
STOP TELLING LIES THAT SOUND KINDA TRUE!!
I DIDN'T BORROW ANYTHING FROM YOU!!

YOU'RE NOT EVEN INVOLVED IN THE TRAINING SO KEEP YOUR MOUTH SHUT!
SHUT UP, PERVERT !!
MAYBE HE JUST DOESN'T HAVE WHAT IT TAKES?
JUST GIVE UP.

I'M NOT A PERV!
SO ARE MOST PERVERTS.
I'M JUST REALLY CURIOUS!!
I'M NOT LIKE YOU!!
IT'S COOL, MAN.
I BORROW IT MYSELF EVERY COUPLE OF DAYS.
BUT I'M NOT A PERV LIKE YOU, ALL RIGHT?!
YEAH, I KNOW !!
I LOOK AT IT TWICE A DAY.
I GUESS IT'S GOING TO TAKE TIME.
A LITTLE OVER TEN SECONDS AFTER ONE MONTH...
WHAT ABOUT YOU?! YOU'RE CURIOUS TOO!
...
WE'VE GOT TWO MORE MONTHS.
THE HÔGYOKU WAKES AT THE END OF DECEMBER...

WE HAVE TO HURRY.
SO LITTLE TIME...

KLAK
TOMP
KLAK

TOMP
TOMP
TOMP
KLAK
KLAK
TOMP
KLAK

KLAK
KRE
EK
ULQUI-ORRA...
...ENTER-ING.

WELCOME...
...ULQUI-ORRA...
...AND YAMMY.

IT...

...WON'T BE LONG NOW.

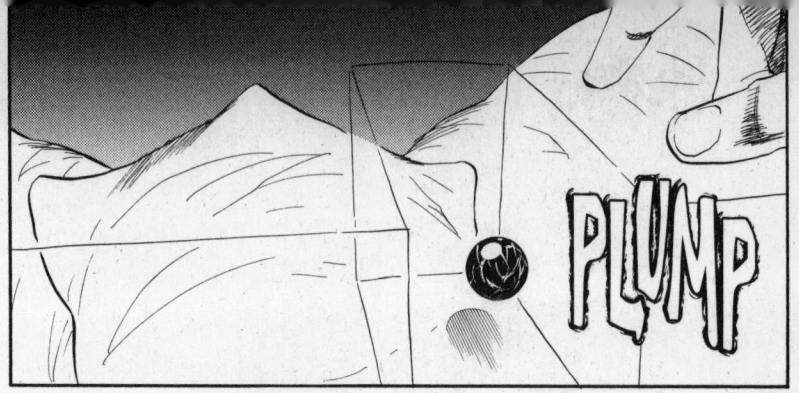
PLUMP

HWOOOOOOO
...EXACTLY WHEN THE SOUL SOCIETY EXPECTS IT TO.
IT WILL AWAKEN...
IT'S AT 50 PER-CENT.
WHAT'S THE STATUS OF THE HÔGYOKU?

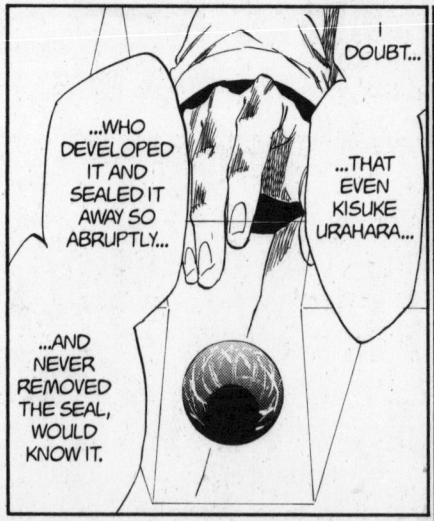
I DOUBT...
...WHO DEVELOPED IT AND SEALED IT AWAY SO ABRUPTLY...
...THAT EVEN KISUKE URAHARA...
...AND NEVER REMOVED THE SEAL, WOULD KNOW IT.

BUT THERE'S A SECRET...
...THAT ONLY THOSE WHO'VE ACTUALLY TOUCHED THE HÔGYOKU KNOW.

...FOR A SHORT TIME...
SWUP
...IS JOINED WITH SOME-ONE WHO POSSESSES TWICE THE SPIRIT ENERGY OF A CAPTAIN...
WHEN THE HŌGYOKU, IN A DORMANT STATE WITH ITS SEAL REMOVED...
KREEK
...IS RELEASED.
...ITS FULL POWER...
KREESH
BOOM
...TELL ME YOUR NAME...
...NEW COMRADE?
CAN YOU...

WONDER-WEISS...
WONDER-WEISS...
MARGERA.
DO YOU REMEMBER THE ORDER...
...I GAVE YOU A MONTH AGO, ULQUIORRA?

CARRY IT OUT.
YES.
THE CHOICE IS YOURS.
TAKE WHOMEVER YOU LIKE.
KLAK
YES, SIR.
WOULD YOU...
...LIKE TO GO TOO...
OH, AND...

...GRIMM-JOW?

SHWUFF

KLANK
KLANK
KLANK
KLANK
KLANK
KLANK
KLANK
KLANK
CRAP! CRAP! CRAP!
CRAP!!
DARN YOU!!
BREAK! BREAK!! BREAK, DARN IT!!
GRAAA

OR I'LL SEND YOU BACK TO THE SOUL SOCIETY !!
SHUT UP AND CONCEN-TRATE!!
WHAM
THWAK
AAAH
THWAM

CAN'T THEY TALK TO THEIR SWORDS MORE QUIETLY?
GEEZ ...

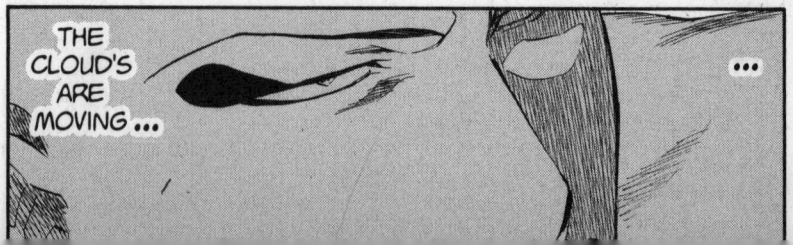
THE CLOUD'S ARE MOVING...
...

NO.
YOU SAY SOMETHING, IKKAKU?
HUH?

IT'S NOTHING.

KR
AK

THANK YOU!
MS. YORU-ICHI!
I PREFER THIS YELLOW ONE...
WHAT?! IT'S HIDEOUS! IT LOOKS LIKE A LITTLE GIRL'S SWIMSUIT!
BUT...AM I OKAY WITH THAT?! I KNOW IT'S MS. YORUICHI, BUT PERHAPS I HAVE TO VOICE AN OPINION SOMETIMES.
BUT WAIT! HOW CAN MS. YORUICHI BE WRONG?!
PINK LAMÉ
THIS ?!
ONE-PIECE

The Seireitei

Training Grounds Behind Thirteenth Company's Barracks

230. Dead White Invasion

THAT'S KUCHIKI AND ONE OF THE RYOKA...
ER...
ORIHIME.
THEY'RE TRAINING FOR THE COMING WAR.
THEY'VE BEEN AT IT A MONTH.

THEY LOOK ...
...LIKE THEY'RE HAVING TOO MUCH FUN.
HEY!
YOU THINK SO TOO?
RUKIA WAS NEVER GOOD AT MAKING FRIENDS.
SHE...
...RARELY OPENS UP.

I WAS SURPRISED WHEN SHE SHOWED UP WITH THAT DESPERATE LOOK AND ASKED ME TO OPEN THE TRAINING GROUNDS BEHIND THE BARRACKS.
SIP

I'M HAPPY FOR HER.
SHE'S FOUND HERSELF A FRIEND.

EVEN IF THAT FRIEND...
...IS A HUMAN?
DON'T SAY THAT.
FORGIVE ME.

THOSE YOUNG PEOPLE ARE UNUSUAL. MAYBE THEY'LL BECOME SOUL REAPERS WHEN THEY REACH THE SOUL SOCIETY.
AND YOU KNOW...
EVEN THOUGH THEY LIVE IN DIFFERENT WORLDS...
...FRIEND-SHIP IS A FINE THING.
NO.
THIS IS GOOD.

OH!
THAT'S RIGHT.
SO, WHAT DID YOU COME HERE FOR?
WAS THERE SOME-THING YOU WANTED?

ELEVENTH COMPANY'S CAPTAIN WON'T WAKE UP AND I DON'T KNOW WHERE THE ASSISTANT CAPTAIN IS.
IT'S CHAOS AROUND HERE. TENTH COMPANY'S IN THE WORLD OF THE LIVING AND...
WHAT ARE YOU DOING WITH THIS?
AND THOSE TWO FROM TWELFTH COMPANY WON'T COME OUT OF THE LAB.
THIS MONTH'S SEIREITEI BULLETIN...
THE MAIL-ORDER CATA-LOGUE'S INSIDE.
SEIREITEI BULLETIN

CAPTAIN TÔSEN NEVER ASKED US TO DO ANYTHING.
I NEVER REALIZED THAT A CAPTAIN'S DUTIES WERE SO DIFFICULT.

SORRY.
I HAVE WORK TO DO.
STAY AWHILE.

I SHOULD BE GOING.
WELL ...

MAYBE ANOTHER TIME.
THOUGH I WOULDN'T MIND WATCHING THOSE TWO TRAIN FOR A WHILE.

FOUR MONTHS, EH?

NOT MUCH TIME TO MEND THE HEART...
...MUCH LESS TO BUILD STRENGTH.

IF ONLY THIS FLEETING PEACE...

...COULD LAST A LITTLE LONGER...

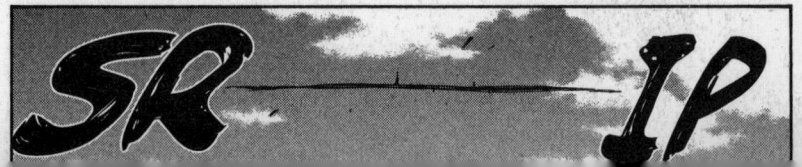
SR IP

KRAK
SKREEK

230. Dead White Invasion

RRMMMMMMMMMMM

ARRAN-CARS ?!
NOW?
AREN'T THEY A LITTLE EARLY?!
THEY'RE DEFINITELY EARLY.
BUT THERE'S NO TIME TO FIGURE OUT WHY.

HEY!
WE PICKED A GOOD SPOT.

MAYBE THEY'RE THE REINFORCEMENTS FROM THE SOUL SOCIETY THAT SIX TOLD US ABOUT.
TAKE A GOOD LOOK. THOSE ARE SOUL REAPERS.

THERE'S SOME GUYS WITH PRETTY HIGH SPIRITUAL PRESSURES DOWN THERE.
WANNA START WITH THEM?

OH...
I'M SORRY.
I MEAN THE FORMER SIX.

RIGHT?

THE GUY I WANNA KILL...
...ISN'T DOWN THERE.
HEY!
WAIT, GRIMMJOW !!

*SOUL REAPERS CALL IT DOOM BLAST.

ALL OF 'EM.
MA...
LET'S GO, ROOKIE!
HEY!
DON'T JUST STAND THERE DROOL-ING!
HMPH...
ANOTHER FREAK JOINS THE TEAM.
AH...
SHOOM

THW
CAPTAIN TÔSHIRÔ HITSUGAYA, TENTH COMPANY!
WHAT A COINCI-DENCE! I'M A TEN TOO.
ARRAN-CAR DIEZ...
YAMMY!

YOU MUST'VE FOUGHT SOMEBODY WITH A BIG MOUTH!
YOU KNOW ABOUT US?
TEN!
THEN YOU'RE AN ESPADA.

SHFF
UH-HUH.
MY NAME'S LUPPI.
...AN ESPADA TOO?
ARE YOU ...

AH...
FWAP FWAP FWAP

I'M RANKED...
...NUMBER SIX-- SEXTA.

...CUT THAT ONE?
CAN I...
FWAP FWAP
...
AH...

LET GO OF ME!!

WELL THIS IS EXACTLY WHAT I'VE BEEN TRAINING FOR TOO!!
IT'S NOW OR NEVER!
THIS IS EXACTLY WHY YOUR PALS FROM THE SOUL SOCIETY ARE HERE!!
LET THEM HANDLE IT!!
YOU'RE NOT READY YET!!

WHAP

LET HIM GO.

SHINJI!
ARE YOU NUTS ?!
C'MON!

I'VE BEEN LOOKING FOR YOU, SOUL REAPER.
HELLO.

SHWIFF
AND I'VE BEEN WAITING FOR YOU.
I WANNA SHOW YOU...
...HOW MUCH I'VE CHANGED ...
...IN THE LAST MONTH.

HEY...
I CAN'T WEAR THAT!
K-KIYONE!
...FOR YOU!!
I FOUND THE PERFECT BATHING SUIT...
ISANE!!
IT'S HARD TO FIND A NICE SWIMSUIT THAT FITS.
IT'S KINDA CUTE, BUT IT'S SO SMALL.
THAT'S NICE.
TMP TMP TMP

231. The Mascaron Drive

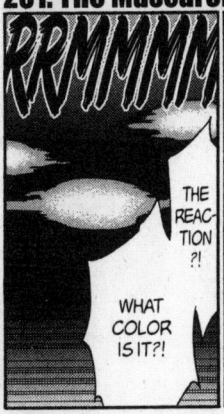

*RESTRICTION REMOVAL

BLEACH 231. The Mascaron Drive

FOUR ARRANCARS HAVE BEEN DETECTED IN NORTH KARAKURA.
THEY ARE BELIEVED TO BE ESPADAS!
THEY'RE ENGAGING THE HITSUGAYA ADVANCE TEAM!!

!

I JUST RECEIVED THE REPORT TOO.
YES, SIR!

KU-CHIKI!

WAIT, RUKIA! I'LL GO WITH YOU!
DASH
YES, SIR!

THE KIDÔ CORPS ARE WORKING ON OPENING THE GATE!
GO TO THE SENKAI-MON IN FRONT OF THE BARRACKS !!

I TOLD YOU WHEN WE CAME HERE...
YOU DON'T HAVE A HELL BUTTERFLY. IF YOU TRY TO PASS THROUGH THE SENKAIMON WITH ME, YOU'LL END UP IN THE DANGAI, THE BORDER BETWEEN THE WORLD OF THE LIVING AND THE SOUL SOCIETY.
NO, ORIHIME.

IT WILL TAKE A LITTLE TIME, BUT YOU'LL BE ABLE TO RETURN TO THE WORLD OF THE LIVING.
I JUST ORDERED THE OUTER WALL TO BE STABILIZED SO YOU CAN SAFELY PASS THROUGH THE DANGAI.
TMP

...ORI-HIME.
DON'T LOOK LIKE THAT...

UNDER-STAND?
I KNOW YOU'RE IN A HURRY, BUT YOU HAVE TO STAY CALM.

YES, SIR.

OKAY.

I'LL BE WAITING ON THE OTHER SIDE.

TMP TMP

THE HÔGYOKU WAS SUPPOSED TO AWAKEN IN THE WINTER!
THIS ISN'T RIGHT. IT'S TOO SOON FOR THE ESPADAS TO SHOW UP!

...HAPPENING?!
WHAT'S...

HA!

KRMMMMMMMMMM
BANKAI, EH?
SO WHAT?

MAYBE YOU FORGOT.
MY BANKAI ATTACK...
DID YOU FOR-GET?
YOUR BANKAI COULDN'T STOP ME.

...GAVE YOU THAT SCAR!

RRRMMM
...GRIMM-JOW.
RRMMM
I'VE GOT A QUESTION FOR YOU...
WHAT HAPPEN-ED...
...TO YOUR ARM?
I GOT RID OF IT.
OH, YEAH?
...TO KILL YOU.
I ONLY NEED ONE ARM...

THEN I GUESS I DON'T HAVE TO...
...HOLD BACK!
IF YOU DO...
...YOU'RE GONNA DIE REAL QUICK.
I CAN STAY HOLLOWFIED FOR EXACTLY ELEVEN SECONDS.
I'LL FINISH HIM BY THEN!
WHOOP
FWOP

WOOOOOO!

DOOM

WHAT'S THAT?!
WHA...?
ZAK
ZAK
ZAK
I DON'T HAVE TIME TO EXPLAIN.
SORRY, MAN.
SHOOM

KRA
UGH...
SPSHHH
WOOM

GETSUGA...
...TENSHÔ!

KR
AK
HUA !!
WHAT WAS THAT ?!
IT WAS NICE AND COOL!
HMPH ...
LOOKS LIKE I'LL HAVE TO PERFORM BANKAI AGAINST HIM EVEN WITH THE GENTEI KAIJO LIFTED.

SHU
SHUT UP.
SWOOOOOOO
DON'T YOU GET IT?
YOU CAN'T BEAT ME ONE ON ONE.
I TOLD YOU...
TWO AGAINST ONE ISN'T MY STYLE.
OR DO I HAVE TO KILL HIM?
WILL YOU TALK TO HIM?
CAN I HAVE THAT BOY?
YAMMY!
WHAT A PAIN ...
NO?

LET'S GO, FOUR ON ONE!
THESE GUYS ARE A JOKE.
...AND TAKE YOU ALL ON.
I'LL RELEASE...
SHUK
HÔTEN
NO WAY!!

LUNK
THAT'S RIGHT.
YES.
B...
BUT ...!
YOU'VE USED UP TOO MUCH ENERGY!
I'LL GO! YOU STAY HERE AND REST!!
AND...
BOTH OF YOU STAY HERE AND REST.
BUT YOU'RE NEARLY EXHAUSTED TOO, RENJI.
TMP
...I'LL GO.

232. The Mascaron Drive 2

BLEACH
ブリーチ

SHH
RELEASE!
ZANPAKU-TÔ...
I WON'T LET YOU!!
SHOOM

KRE-KK
BANKAI !!
DAIGUREN HYÔRIN-MARU!!

...TREPADORA!
(IVY MAIDEN)
STRANGLE HIM...
SHWA
P
!
SWU
P
KA
NK
HMPH!

KRS

KRLLK
THAT'S YOUR RELEASE ATTACK?
WHAT'S WRONG ?
IS THAT IT?
SKRSHHHHHHH
BOMMMMMMM
GOOD JOB!
HA HA!
WHAT IF THAT ATTACK...
BUT...
YOU CAPTAINS AREN'T TOO SHABBY.
YOU SUR-PRISED ME!
I REALLY DIDN'T THINK YOU COULD STOP IT.

...WERE EIGHT TIMES STRONGER?

READ THIS WAY
...TIMES?
EIGHT...

KIR
OOM
CAPTAIN !!
DARN...
SEE?
...IT.
I TOLD YOU TO FIGHT ME FOUR AGAINST ONE!

SORRY.
OH.
I MEAN...
...FOUR AGAINST EIGHT.
THWOOSH
SHWOOOOOOOOD

HUFF
HUFF
HUFF
THIS...
...ISN'T...
...SOUL REAPER POWER.
HOW?

FWIK
...IN ONLY A MONTH?!
HOW DID YOU DO IT...
SHO
DM
I TOLD YOU...
WH
AM

I DON'T HAVE TIME TO EXPLAIN.
FWOOSH
SHWAK

WHO
OF
WHAN
YOU...
Y...
...LITTLE JERK !!
DOOM BLAST !!

THWANG
GRAAAAAH...
AH...
RKMMMMMMM

BUG
HMPH!
KA
IT'S OVER ...
...GRIMM-JOW.

MY MASK !!!

IT'S OVER...
SOUL REAPER !!
SHW
AK

I'M SORRY.
YES, MA'AM ...
Y...
... ISANE.
BU... BUT, CAPTAIN ...!
GO WITH THAT ONE...
WHAT'S THE DIFFERENCE? WHY DON'T YOU GO WITH THAT ONE, ISANE?
SFX
I'VE DECIDED ON THIS ONE.
WHAT'S THE DIFFERENCE?!

233. El Violador

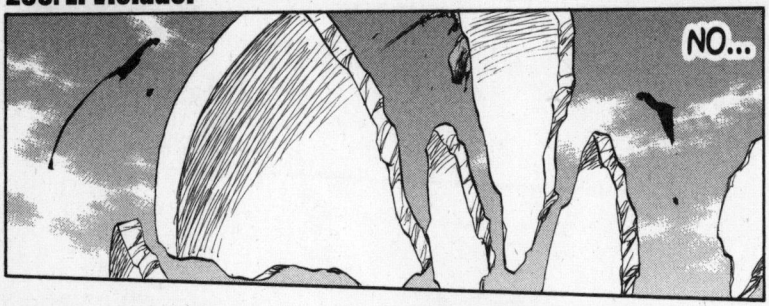

KRANG
LOOKS LIKE...
...YOU USED UP ALL YOUR POWER.
YOU GOT SHORT OF BREATH THE INSTANT YOUR MASK CAME OFF!
IT'S OVER, SOUL REAPER!
I'M HURT PRETTY BAD MYSELF, BUT...
...IN THE END, EVEN WITH THAT POWER OF YOURS...
YOU COULDN'T...
...BEAT ME!!

BLEACH. 233. El Violador

SHWAK
WHAM
WHAM
WHAM
WHAM
WHAM
WHAM

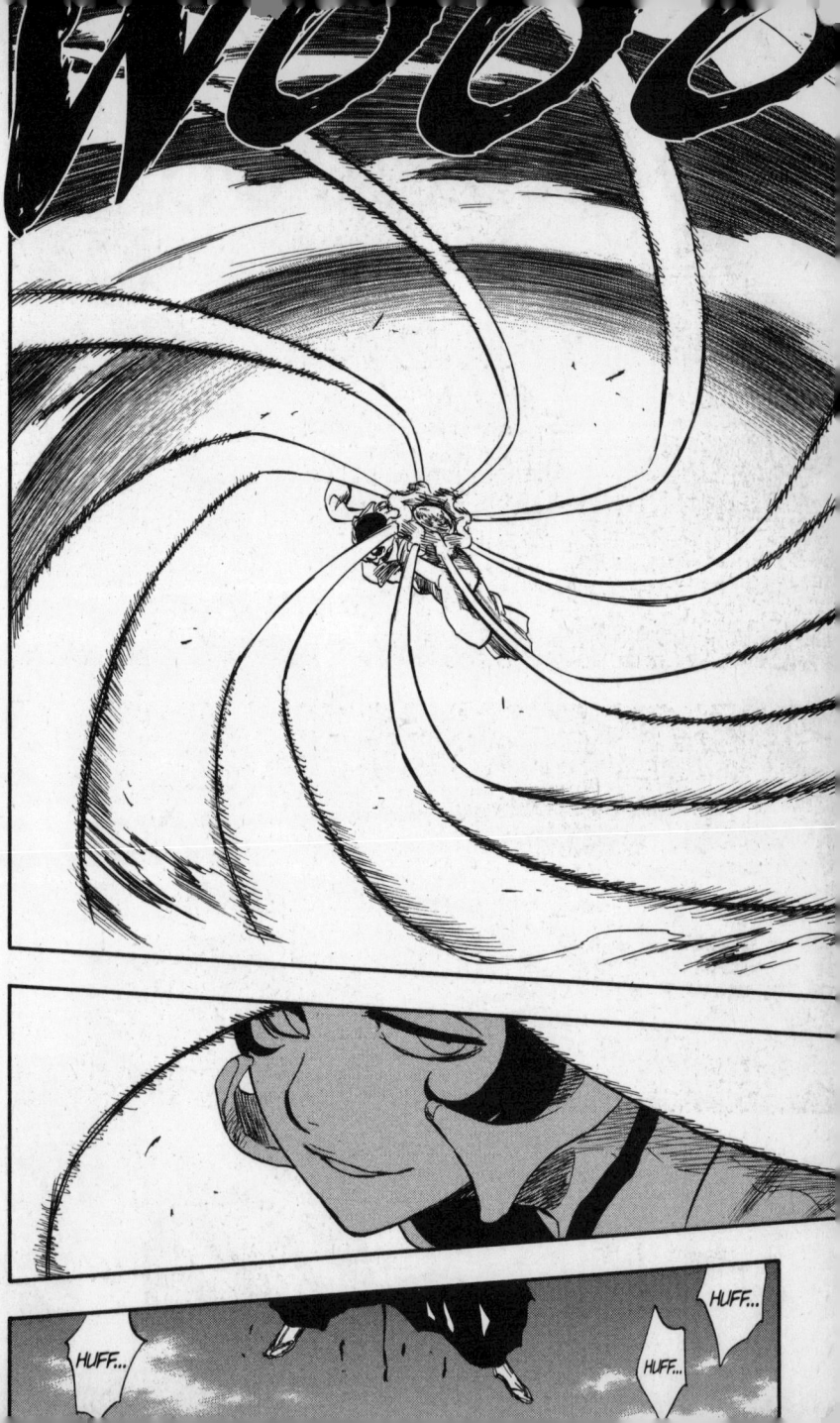
HUFF...
HUFF...
HUFF...

DO
OM
WHUP
ARE YOU GUYS REALLY OFFICERS OF THE THIRTEEN COURT GUARD COMPANIES?
WHUP
WHUP
GEEZ...
THIS IS PATHETIC.
THW
IP
-RING.
BOOO-

WOOSH

YAAAAWN...
BUT IT'S A PAIN TO GO LOOK FOR OTHER ONES.

THAT LUPPI STOLE THOSE SOUL REAPERS FROM ME.
UGH...
THERE'S NOTHING TO DO...

WMM

HEY!
ROOKIE!
WHAT'RE YOU DOING?!

WHAP
WWWW
HUH?
...
OH...
WMM
WMM
AHH
URGH !!
I'VE GOT NOTHING TO DO!
STILL

UGH!!
YUMICHIKA!! MATSU-MOTO!!
SHWAP
AGH!!
KREK
WHUP
IT'S LUSCIOUS.
WOW...
YOU'VE GOT A KILLER BODY.
YOU KNOW WHAT, LADY?

!
MAYBE I'LL...
...POKE IT FULL OF HOLES.

SHAK
!
PHEW ...
JUST IN TIME.
KLUNK
THAT WAS CLOSE.
...
WHO ARE YOU?

OH!
FORGIVE ME. I SHOULD INTRODUCE MYSELF.

I'M KISUKE URAHARA.

FWOOO
I'M DE-LIGHTED ...
...TO MAKE YOUR ACQUAIN-TANCE.
I RUN A DINKY LITTLE CANDY STORE CALLED URAHARA SHÔTEN.

SLAK
SKRSHHHHS
WHOA.
THAT ONE'S KIND OF WEIRD.
AH!
AH...
WHUP
!

BOOM
THE OUTER WALL OF THE DANGAI HAS BEEN STABIL-IZED!
YOU CAN PASS THROUGH NOW!!
MS. INOUE!
MS. ORIHIME INOUE!
TMP
!
THANK YOU!
DASH
THANK YOU SO MUCH!!

IT'S CUSTOMARY FOR TWO SOUL REAPERS WITH THEIR HELL BUTTERFLIES REMOVED TO ACCOMPANY A GUEST THROUGH THE PASSAGE!
YOU'RE NOT A RYOKA ANYMORE. YOU'RE OUR GUEST!
NO, THAT'S OKAY...
HUH ?!
WE'LL ESCORT YOU.
I KNOW IT'S A NUISANCE, BUT PLEASE INDULGE US!

I KNOW I CAN HELP OUT NOW!
IT'S OKAY. I GOT A LITTLE STRONGER OVER THE LAST MONTH.
I'D BETTER HURRY...

THANKS.
THEN ...
OKAY ...

AND EVERYONE ELSE!
SO HOLD ON, ICHIGO...

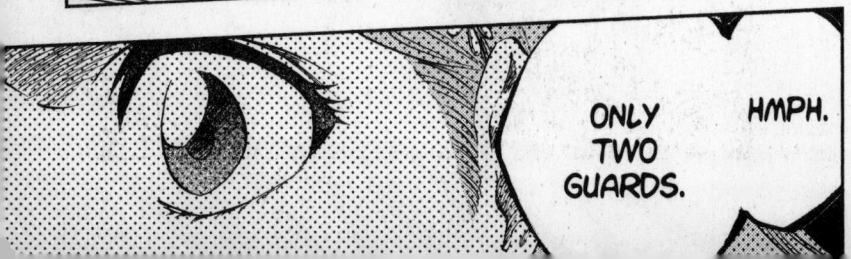
ONLY TWO GUARDS.
HMPH.

WHO
OH
KRE
EK
RIP
THESE SOUL REAPERS ARE MORE...
...IN-COMPETENT THAN I THOUGHT.
THEY DON'T SEEM TO REALIZE...
...THAT THE PASSAGE IS THE MOST DANGEROUS PART.

CONTI
NUED
IN
BLEACH
27

WHO ARE THESE FOOLS?
WHAT'S THIS?

South San Francisco Public Library
[redacted]
3 9048 08240484 3

Next Volume Previe

SSF

Orih
her a
aband

Rec

S.S.F. Public Library
West Orange
840 West Orange Ave.
South San Francisco, CA 94080

MAR 2009

GAYLORD